Dream
Interpretation

The Joy of
Dream
Interpretation

Eili Goldberg

Astrolog Publishing House

Cover Design: Na'ama Yaffe
Language Consultants: Marion Duman, Carole Koplow
Layout and Graphics: Daniel Akerman
Production Manager: Dan Gold

Astrolog Publishing House
P.O. Box 1123, Hod Hasharon 45111, Israel
Tel: 972-9-7412044
Fax: 972-9-7442714
E-Mail: info@astrolog.co.il
Astrolog Web Site: www.astrolog.co.il

Published by Astrolog Publishing House 2002

10 9 8 7 6 5 4 3 2 1

Abandonment If the dreamer is abandoned, this signifies a quarrel with a friend. If he abandons another person, it means that he will renew a contact with a friend.

Abundance This is a clear indication that the dreamer will have a life filled with prosperity and wealth.

Abyss Looking down into an abyss is a sign that the dreamer is about to encounter danger.

Accident A traffic accident signifies that a bad decision will lead to an unsuccessful deal. If one dreams about an accident occurring in an unknown place, it indicates an unsuccessful love life. Dreaming about being involved in a railroad accident is an indication of exaggerated self-confidence. If the dreamer is in a plane crash, it is a warning against bad business deals in the near future.

Accordion When the dreamer is playing the accordion, it is a sign that he will soon marry. If the sound of the instrument can only be heard and not seen, disappointment can be expected. Off-key music or notes indicate depression and despondency.

Accountant Dreaming about an accountant is connected to the dreamer's financial problems. A conversation with an accountant means that the dreamer has a strong desire to raise his standard of living.

Acrobat This signifies that the dreamer has a dangerous enemy of whom he is not aware. If an acrobat falls in the dream, it indicates that a plot has been foiled. If the dreamer himself is the acrobat, it means that he needs reinforcement from his surroundings.

Actor An actor on the stage indicates two-faced behavior on the part of one of the dreamer's friends.

Adam and Eve Such a dream signifies a person seeking the virginal or primal aspect of life, or an individual who lives a full life, in harmony with himself.

Adultery Indicates a guilty conscience regarding the dreamer's sexuality.

Age If the dreamer himself or others close to him appear older than they are in reality, or if in the dream the dreamer is worried about his age, it means that he will become ill in the near future. If the dreamer or others close to him appear younger than in reality, it is advisable for the dreamer to avoid coming into conflict with those around him.

Agreement This suggests that the dreamer's problems will be solved and his worries will disappear completely.

Albatross The dreamer will overcome obstacles and reach his desired objective.

Alcoholic Beverages If the dreamer is drinking alcoholic beverages, it means that he must beware of being misled.

Almonds Eating almonds predicts a journey to distant places.

Amusement Being amused or in a good mood in a dream means that the dreamer will soon have good luck. Dreaming about some kind of entertainment means that an opportunity is about to present itself, and it would be a shame to miss it.

Anchor This symbolizes stability, security and earthiness. The dreamer has both feet firmly planted on the ground.

Angel This is an indication of the dreamer's strong belief in a superior power; he makes no attempt to alter his own destiny. It also signifies a successful marriage.

Anger This portends good and significant news for the dreamer. Anger at a person known to the dreamer indicates that the person does not deserve the dreamer's trust. Anger at an unknown person indicates that the dreamer's life will soon change for the better.

Animals The meaning changes according to the type of animal. (Refer to the name of the particular animal.)

Animal Young/Cubs If animal young appear with their mother in a dream, it indicates maternal feelings. Wild animal cubs symbolize a longing for happiness. Domesticated animal young are indicative of the dreamer's childish personality.

Ankle If the dreamer's ankle appears in the dream, it means success and the solving of problems. If his spouse's ankle appears, it indicates that the dreamer is being unfaithful to her, or the opposite.

Annoyance If the dreamer expresses annoyance or anger, it is a sign that his life will be happy and successful.

Ants A dream about ants suggests that the dreamer reorganize his professional life and make changes in it. Ants that are particularly tiresome indicate an imminent period of frustration and disappointment.

Appetite A large appetite for food and drink is a sign of great sexual passion.

Apple Eating an apple in a dream predicts a rosy future. If the apple is sour, it is a sign that the dreamer will soon be disappointed or experience failure.

Apricot Dreaming about apricots or about eating them indicates a good future and success in most areas of life, with the exception of romance.

Arm A strong arm signifies unexpected success. A weak arm means a great disappointment in the life of the dreamer.

Artichoke This suggests faulty communication with one's partner, as well as disagreements and the lack of ability to understand him/her.

Artist Dreams about artists, painters or other creative people actually indicate the contrary: the dreamer does not have artistic talent and would do better to pursue other avenues of development.

Asparagus This signifies correct and good decisions made by the dreamer. He should continue to follow his heart and not listen to the advice of others.

Astronomer/Astrologer This shows that the dreamer is facing the future with hope and positive expectations.

Auction If a man dreams about an auction, it is a sign that his business will flourish. If a woman dreams about an auction, it means that she will be wealthy and live a life of affluence.

Aura If the aura encircles the dreamer himself, it is a warning of a threat to his status and image.

Avalanche If the dreamer is caught in an avalanche, it means good things are coming his way. If other people are caught in an avalanche, it is a sign that the dreamer is longing to move to a different place.

Avenue An avenue of trees symbolizes ideal love. An avenue of trees shedding their leaves signifies a difficult life full of obstacles.

Avocado This signifies economic success and an improvement in the dreamer's status in the work place.

Ax An ax signifies the end of a family feud, fight or struggle. A sharp ax symbolizes progress; a blunt ax means that business will become slow.

B

Baby Dreaming about an especially happy baby indicates that the dreamer will enjoy true love. Dreaming about a pretty baby predicts true friendship. Dreaming about a sick baby is a sign that the dreamer has treacherous friends.

Bachelorhood If a married person dreams about bachelorhood, it indicates a secret wish to be unfaithful to his/her spouse.

Back Door If the dreamer sees himself entering and leaving through a back door, it indicates an urgent need to effect changes in his life. If he sees another person leaving though the back door, he can expect a financial loss, and it is not advisable to enter into a business partnership.

Badger This indicates the fear that someone else is harvesting the fruits of the dreamer's labors.

Bag/Handbag This predicts the advent of good tidings and significant news concerning the dreamer's future.

Baker/Cook This suggests that the dreamer does not have a clear conscience or is involved in some kind of scam; it reveals a desire to conceal a situation into which the dreamer is being coerced.

Ball (dance) Participating in a ball indicates that the dreamer will have a happy and joyous life, full of love.

Ball (game) If the dreamer is playing ball, it is a sign that he will soon receive good news. If the dreamer sees other people playing ball, it is a sign that he harbors an unhealthy jealousy toward one of his friends.

Ballet This signifies betrayal, envy and quarrels.

Balloon This indicates severe disappointments in the future. A large-than-usual balloon suggests ambitiousness. A balloon plunging from high above signifies regression.

Bananas Bananas suggest that the dreamer is bored at work and is not exploiting his talents. Dreaming about eating a banana indicates a health problem.

Bandage Wearing a bandage is a sign that the dreamer has loyal friends on whom he may depend.

Banking Dreaming about being in a bank indicates business problems. If the dreamer meets the bank manager, it hints at bankruptcy. Money bills in a dream mean financial prosperity.

Banquet/Feast Dreaming about a banquet with many participants predicts a quarrel with one's partner. If the dreamer is single, it indicates marriage in the near future, but one that will end in failure.

Bar (for drinking) This indicates insecurity and a yearning for a better future. A bar with a bartender signifies that the dreamer is longing to throw a party.

Barbecue This signifies that the dreamer is under extreme emotional pressure and is doing nothing to change the situation.

Barbershop/Beauty Parlor If the dreamer is getting his hair cut, it means that he is an ambitious person. The dream is also indicative of a strong character and a person who enjoys standing up for his rights and principles.

Barefoot If the dreamer is barefoot, it is a sign that his path will be fraught with obstacles, but he will overcome them all.

Basket (woven) An overflowing, woven straw basket is a sign of social and financial success. An empty basket, however, symbolizes disappointment, sadness and depression.

Bath Dreaming about taking a bath indicates success in business. If the water is not clear, there might be problems and difficulties in the near future.

Bat (animal) This is a warning about the advent of bad news.

Beach/Shore This means that the dreamer needs some peace and quiet, some respite from the intensive life he leads.

Bear When a bear appears in a dream, the dreamer will have to work hard before he sees the fruits of his labor. Killing a bear symbolizes overcoming obstacles on the path to attaining a certain goal.

Beard A beard in a dream attests to the fact that the dreamer has a strong character and plenty of self-confidence (particularly a white beard).

Bed Almost any situation in which a bed is seen in a dream predicts good things. Making the dreamer's bed indicates marriage in the near future. Making a stranger's bed symbolizes a new and surprising turning-point in life. An unmade bed indicates that the dreamer has problems with sexuality and marriage.

Bed-Linen/Sheets Clean bed-linen means that the dreamer will soon receive good news from far away. Dirty bed-linen indicates financial losses or health problems.

Bedroom This is usually connected to eroticism and sex. At times, it speaks of a positive turning-point in life.

Bee A bee or bees in a dream signify that a joyous occasion is soon to take place in the family. It also means that the dreamer has good friends.

Dream Interpretation

Beehive This indicates a wedding, birth or engagement in the near future.

Beetle The dreamer can expect a brilliant future. He will become important and famous.

Beggar If the dreamer helps a beggar, it means that he should expect good things in all areas of life. If the dreamer refuses to help the beggar, a loss is predicted.

Bell The ringing of a bell in a dream portends bad news concerning a distant acquaintance.

Belt The dreamer will soon receive a large sum of money unexpectedly.

Bicycle This indicates a frenzied lifestyle and the need to slow down. Riding downhill warns of danger in the near future. Riding uphill signifies a rosy future.

Billiards A billiard table with people around it indicates unexpected problems. An isolated pool table indicates that the dreamer should beware of those conspiring against him.

Bills If the dreamer himself is paying bills, it is a sign that his financial concerns will disappear shortly without a trace. Worrying about not having paid bills means that the dreamer's enemies are spreading malicious gossip about him.

Billy-Goat This is the symbol of a demon, the devil or an evil spirit.

Birds If a rich man dreams of birds in flight, it is a sign that he will suffer financial losses. If a poor man or one with financial problems dreams of birds, it is a sign of economic abundance. A wounded bird means that a member of the dreamer's family will cause him harm.

Bird's Nest An empty bird's nest predicts problems. A nest containing eggs indicates a rosy future.

Birth (of animals) This indicates that the dreamer has enemies who are acting behind his back; however, he will overcome this obstacle and succeed in attaining his goals and objectives.

Birth (of people) If a single person dreams about birth, it signifies that certain problems will soon be solved. If a married person dreams about birth, it is a sign that he will soon get pleasant surprises.

Biscuit/Cookie This indicates that the dreamer has the tendency to blame others for his own mistakes and deeds.

Blackberries These warn of financial disappointment or loss of economic status.

Blacksmith It is quite rare to dream about a blacksmith. However, it indicates a spirit torn in two.

Blame If the dreamer is being blamed for something, it suggests that he will be involved in a quarrel in the future. If the dreamer blames someone else, it means that he will quarrel with his associates.

Blanket This indicates good times and a happy life: the thicker and more elaborately decorated the blanket, the happier the dreamer's life will be.

Blaze Flames or a blaze indicate the eruption of bottled-up rage. Overcoming a blaze means that the dreamer will soon receive unexpected good news.

Bleeding This warns of health problems which must be attended to.

Blindfold A blindfold suggests that the dreamer was greatly disappointed by himself and by those around him.

Blindness If the dreamer appears blind in a dream, he is not totally satisfied with his choice of a spouse. If he dreams about leading someone who is blind, it is a sign that he is too dependent on someone who does not actually deserve his trust.

Blood This indicates an unwanted relationship, a quarrel, anger, disagreements or disappointment (particularly in emotional contexts).

Boat This heralds changes for the better in the dreamer's life. A boat on calm waters indicates a change in work place or residence. Rowing a boat is a sign of social success as well as recognition from professional colleagues. If a boat overturns, it is a sign that the dreamer will soon receive important news. A boat on land means significant financial losses.

Book Dreaming about a book signifies great success connected with reading or studying, which will lead the dreamer to a fulfilling and financially rewarding profession. Reading a book in a dream means that the dreamer will go on a trip which will have great significance in his life.

Bouquet (of flowers) This indicates that the dreamer feels that his talents are not appreciated.

Bow and Arrow The dreamer is aware of his talents and has great self-esteem. He knows how to rely on himself and his powers of judgment.

Bowl A full bowl predicts quarrels or disagreements with a partner. An empty bowl is a sign of tranquillity, quiet and rest.

Box/Chest A closed box means financial problems. An open box signifies that a secret, which the dreamer has jealously guarded until now, is about to be revealed. A box that has been broken into indicates licentiousness. A sealed box is a sign of morality.

Bracelet Wearing a bracelet on one's wrist predicts marriage in the near future.

Bread This signifies that the dreamer is satisfied with himself and derives pleasure from his family. Eating bread predicts good health.

Breakage Any kind of breakage in a dream — no matter who is doing the breaking — portends bad things, mainly health problems.

Dream Interpretation

Breakfast This indicates that the individual is going to face a difficult test, and that he fears failure.

Bride This is an indication of virginity, and a lack of maturity and experience of life.

Bridge Crossing a bridge indicates exaggerated concerns which will soon pass. A bridge which collapses is a warning of economic problems. An endless bridge signifies unrequited love. Passing underneath a bridge means that the dreamer must be patient if he is ever to solve his problems.

Broom If the dreamer is sweeping with a broom, it indicates a professional turning point. A broom lying on the ground portends imminent separation from a close friend.

Brother/Sister A dream about a sibling must be interpreted according to the character traits of the dreamer's family.

Building If the dreamer is standing next to a luxurious building, it predicts good and pleasant times. If the dreamer enters the building, it means a loss of control, as well as nervousness and impatience.

Bull If a woman dreams about a bull, it is a sign that she is not sexually satisfied. If a man dreams about a bull, it means he relates brutally to women.

Bundle This warns the dreamer of a great disappointment in the near future.

Burglary Dreaming about a break-in or burglary means that someone whom the dreamer has trusted implicitly is not worthy of such trust.

Burial Contrary to what it seems, burial predicts birth or marriage.

Burn If the dreamer gets burnt, it means he will soon win a large sum of money. If he sees another person getting burnt, it means he will soon make a new friend.

Butter Dreaming about butter means that the dreamer is not focused, and instead of concentrating his efforts in one field, he spreads himself thinly over too many areas and does not succeed in any.

Butterfly This indicates that the dreamer is involved in a passionate love affair.

Buttons Wooden buttons predict success following considerable effort. Pearl buttons foretell a trip in the near future. Fabric buttons indicate that the dreamer's health is deteriorating and he must look after himself. Losing buttons in a dream signifies family problems as a result of financial losses. Finding a button in a dream signifies a promotion at work and prosperity in business.

C

Cabbage This attests to the dreamer's lazy nature, a characteristic which significantly influences the achievements in his life.

Cage If a single woman dreams about a cage, it is a sign that she will soon receive a proposal of marriage. If a man dreams about a cage, it means that he will get married prematurely. Two birds in a cage indicate a wonderful and happy married life.

Cake Dreaming about a cake, particularly a festively decorated cake, indicates good health and happiness.

Calendar This warns the dreamer that he underestimates important issues and disparages other people, and this may very likely have a boomerang effect.

Calling by name When the dreamer is called by name or calls another by name, it is a sign that he will soon enter a good period regarding romance and marriage.

Camel This portends a good future. The dreamer will overcome obstacles with the help of good friends.

Camping Dreaming about sleeping outdoors warns against routine and signifies the need for a vacation. Dreaming about going to an army camp predicts marriage in the near future.

Dream Interpretation

Canal Dreaming about a canal of murky water is an indication of problems and worries. Clear water in a canal signifies that problems will soon be solved. Weeds growing in a canal warn of financial embroilment. Falling into a canal indicates a drop in status. Jumping over a canal means the dreamer will maintain his self-respect.

Candlesticks A good sign: changes for the better in one's life, or participation in happy occasions and financial success.

Candy/Sweets A box full of candy predicts that the dreamer's economic situation is about to improve. If a woman dreams of receiving a box of candies, it is a sign that she has a secret admirer. If the dreamer sends a box of candy to another person, it predicts a disappointment.

Cannibal This is an indication of pressure, anxiety, or fears plaguing the dreamer. It is also possible that the dreamer is not physically healthy.

Cannibalism This indicates a tendency toward self-destruction and loss of self-control.

Cannon This predicts war, conflict or quarrels.

Cape If the dreamer is wearing a cape, it is a sign that he inspires a feeling of confidence in his friends. If another person is wearing a cape, it is a sign that the dreamer deems him highly trustworthy.

Captain Dreaming about a captain (of a boat or airplane) attests to the dreamer's ambitious nature and his desire to rule and lead others.

Dream Interpretation

Car Any kind of dream about a car means good things: problems will be solved, complications will sort themselves out and life will flow smoothly.

Caravan This indicates that the dreamer will embark on a journey in the near future, and that he must beware of physical harm.

Cards Winning a card game is a prediction of marriage in the near future. Losing a card game signifies that the dreamer will soon be forced to take risks.

Carpentry This signifies that the dreamer is bored with his profession or occupation and needs variety.

Carpet Walking on a carpet indicates a love of luxury. Cleaning a carpet means personal problems in one's domestic or romantic life.

Carrot This signifies that the dreamer is not coping with his problems and chooses to ignore them.

Cat This is an indication of cunning, subversion, lack of trust and treachery. The dream urges the dreamer to examine his friends and confidants carefully.

Cattle This indicates financial success in the near future. It attests to the dreamer's conservative personality and tendency to calculate his every step.

Cauliflower The dreamer can expect quiet times and a calm period in his life.

Cave If the dreamer is hiding in a cave, it is a sign that someone is spreading vicious rumors about him and wishes to cause him harm.

Celebration/Party If the dreamer is enjoying a celebration or party, it is a sign of good things to come. A dream of a formal party — without dancing or warmth — is a sign that the dreamer has made several mistakes for which he must now pay the price.

Celery This means that only good things will come the way of the dreamer, bringing abundance, happiness and joy into his life.

Cellar This indicates a loss of the dreamer's self-confidence. Dreaming about a wine-cellar represents a warning against marrying a gambler.

Cement Any form of cement in a dream means a change for the better or an improvement in the dreamer's financial status.

Cemetery This indicates that good news is on the way, or that a sick friend is recovering. A dream of the death of a family member predicts a period of stress and problems.

Cereal/Porridge This warns of dangerous enemies that may embroil the dreamer.

Chain A good sign. Wearing a gold or silver chain predicts that the dreamer will receive a gift from an admirer or lover. Dreaming about the clasp of a chain indicates that the dreamer's problems will soon be solved.

Chair If someone is sitting on the chair, it heralds the arrival of another person bringing money. An empty chair signifies that the dreamer is about to receive news from a friend abroad.

Champion/Championship This indicates that the dreamer is ambitious and competitive, and will do anything to attain his goals.

Charity Receiving charity is a sign that the dreamer's financial status will deteriorate slightly, but not significantly. Giving charity in a dream is a sign of improvement in his financial status.

Cheese (hard, yellow) This indicates that the dreamer has a difficult character and an uncompromising stubbornness that alienates his friends.

Cherries These represent good-naturedness and loyalty and predict good things. Eating cherries is a sign that one's wishes are about to come true.

Chess If the dreamer is playing chess, he can expect to have a serious quarrel with a friend or relative, with bitter consequences. A chessboard means that the dreamer will meet new people as a result of a crisis which he has undergone.

Chest (body) Whether it is a man's or a woman's chest, it is a symbol of an intimate relationship with a person who is close.

Chick For those involved in agriculture and breeding chickens, this predicts damage. For others, it indicates that they count their chickens before they're hatched, and should be more realistic.

Children If a woman dreams about children, it means that she is satisfied with her family life. If a man dreams about children, it means that he can expect a period of quiet with regard to his domestic life.

Chiming of a Clock This image always heralds good things: the louder the chiming, the happier life will be.

Chimney This predicts success. A smoking chimney heralds good tidings coming the way of the dreamer. A broken chimney is a foreboding of worries and problems.

Chrysanthemum This usually symbolizes love or deep affection.

Cigarettes If someone lights a cigarette for the dreamer, it means that the latter will soon need assistance from another person. If a cigarette butt appears in an ashtray, it indicates the inability to fulfill hopes and desires.

Cleanliness A dream about the cleanliness of objects means that the dreamer will soon have to shoulder an unbearable burden and experience feelings of extreme oppression.

Climb Any type of climb — up a mountain, a ladder, etc. — means that the dreamer will overcome all the obstacles that stand in the way of attaining his objectives.

Clock Any sort of clock attests to the dreamer's achievement-oriented character, or to his actual achievements; it also symbolizes wealth and abundance.

Clothing A closet full of clothing means that the dreamer can soon expect problems in different areas. If he is partially dressed, he is able to attain his objective. Getting dressed in a dream means progress. Getting undressed means regression. If the dreamer is dressed eccentrically, it indicates substantial success.

Clover Because of the shape of its leaves, clover symbolizes a fork in the dreamer's path.

Clown This shows that the dreamer is living a dishonest and deceitful life. Masks mean that one is two-faced.

Coat Almost any context in which a coat appears (worn, sold or bought) indicates that a certain investment will pay off and the dreamer will benefit from it. Wearing a coat that belongs to someone else means that the dreamer needs help from that person. Losing a coat in a dream indicates that the dreamer should be cautious when making any business decisions.

Cobra This is a sign of serious sexual problems (particularly in the case of men).

Coffee This means that the dreamer is under emotional pressure and suffers from tension in his daily life.

Coins A gold coin indicates that the dreamer has gone out to enjoy nature. A worn coin predicts a dreary day. A copper coin means a heavy burden and serious responsibility. A shining coin means success in romance.

Collar If the collar is tight around the dreamer's

neck, it signifies that he is afraid of a strong person who intimidates him.

Colors All the colors of the spectrum, except black, are a good sign. Bright colors — security and tranquillity; white — innocence and purity; blue — overcoming problems with the help of one's friends; yellow — high expectations; orange or gray — one must have patience; red — social events; green — envy; brown — good news; pink — a surprise; black — bad moods and depression.

Comb If the dreamer is combing his hair, it means that a sick friend needs his help.

Compass This symbolizes loyalty: the dreamer has loyal friends who will come to his aid in times of trouble.

Conference (business) This means that the dreamer's financial situation will improve.

Confusion Chaos and disorder in a dream warn of accidents and obstacles. One should be more alert.

Contest/Competition This means that the dreamer must resist strong temptation.

Conversation A conversation between the dreamer and another person indicates difficulties that may arise at work or in business, such as theft, damage, etc.

Cooking This is usually connected with sexuality. The different stages of cooking — before, during and after — are parallel to the past, present and future in the dreamer's life. Dreaming about cooking also warns of health problems.

Coral This warns against taking a particular step in any area of life.

Corpse This indicates that the dreamer is dealing with death, the occult or infinity. If a businessman dreams of a corpse, it means that his reputation will be ruined, he will fail in business or go bankrupt. If a young man dreams of a corpse, it suggests unrequited love.

Corridor If an unknown corridor appears in a dream, it is a sign that the dreamer must make an important decision which is not influenced by external factors.

Crabs Crabs symbolize good health. A single crab symbolizes betrayal.

Crib An empty crib speaks of a lack of confidence or health problems. Rocking a baby in a crib indicates marital problems.

Crime An encounter with a criminal in a dream warns of questionable individuals. If the dreamer himself appears as a criminal, it is a sign that he is not sufficiently aware of the hardships of others.

Crocodile This signifies that someone close to the dreamer is behaving in an exceptionally friendly manner; however, beneath this hearty exterior, he is plotting to harm him.

Crying Crying in a dream generally heralds good tidings and indicates that there will be reasons for rejoicing and celebrating. However, at times, it may be seen as a signal of distress from a friend.

Cucumber The dreamer will become ill with a serious disease in the near future.

Cup A cup full of liquid is a sign of good luck. An empty cup signifies shortage. A dark-colored cup indicates problems at work or in business. A light-colored cup symbolizes a bright future. A cup out of which liquid has spilled predicts fighting and tension in the family.

Currants (red) The dreamer is avoiding someone whom he is unable to confront. Picking currents is an indication of the dreamer's optimistic personality: the ability always to look on the bright side.

Cursing If the dreamer curses, it suggests that his goals and objectives will be attained after a particularly big effort. If the dreamer is being cursed by someone else, it means that there are enemies conspiring against him.

Dream Interpretation

Curtain Closing a curtain in a dream means that people who are close to the dreamer are plotting against him and deceiving him.

Cutting This indicates an unhealthy connection with someone close to the dreamer. Cutting oneself indicates family problems.

Cyclamen For men, a dream about this flower symbolizes impotence. For women, it signifies the inability to forge healthy relationships with men.

Daffodil A daffodil indicates that the dreamer suffers from problems relating to his sexual identity.

Dagger This signifies that the dreamer does not trust those around him.

Daisy A daisy predicts good times accompanied by happiness and inner confidence.

Dancing This is a sign of vitality, love of the good life, sexiness and health.

Danger This signifies success: the greater the danger in the dream, the greater the success in reality.

Darkness The appearance of darkness, or walking in the dark, indicates that the dreamer is distressed, confused and restless.

Dark-Skinned Person Dreaming about a dark-skinned person suggests that the dreamer does not have tension and excitement in his life. It may also indicate that he has difficulties resulting from sexual tension.

Dates (fruit) These predict the marriage of the dreamer or of one of his close friends in the near future.

Deafness A symbol: What we do not know cannot hurt us!

Death Contrary to what one might expect, dreaming about death heralds a long and good life. Dreaming about the death of person who is actually ill means that he will recover soon.

Deer This symbolizes the father figure or the desire to resemble someone who is close to you and who constitutes an authority figure.

Depression Dreaming about depression indicates the opposite: the dreamer will have a golden opportunity to extricate himself from his present situation and improve his life unrecognizably.

Desert If the dreamer is walking in the desert, it predicts a journey. If a storm breaks out during the dream, it means that the journey will not be satisfactory. If the dreamer is in the desert and is suffering from hunger and thirst, it means he needs to invigorate his life.

Devil This actually foretells an easier and better future.

Diamond This signifies domestic quarrels or confusion and disorder in the dreamer's family life.

Diary This symbolizes excessive acquisitiveness or a pathological jealousy of someone close to the dreamer.

Dice Dice symbolize gambling. If the dreamer's financial situation is actually good, it means that he will profit substantially from gambling, and vice versa.

Digestion Dreaming about the digestive system, one of its components or the sensations connected to it, indicates health problems. (See also Digestive System).

Digestive System Any dream concerning the digestive system (including vomiting and diarrhea) is a sign of health or nutritional problems.

Dirt Dreaming about dirt, particularly if it appears on clothing, means that certain health problems must be attended to. Dreaming about falling into dirt or garbage predicts that the dreamer will move house in the near future. (See also Stains.)

Disabled Person/Cripple Any dream about a disabled person (the nature or level of disability is irrelevant) attests to the fact that the dreamer's conscience is urging him to help others less fortunate than himself.

Disaster This is an indication of enemies plotting against the dreamer, particularly in the workplace, and advises him to seek protection from them.

Distress If the dreamer is in distress, it is a sign that his financial situation will improve substantially.

Divorce Some claim that dreaming about divorce indicates sexual problems. If the dreamer is married, it means that he is happily married. If a single person who has a partner dreams about divorce, it means that he feels insecure about the relationship.

Doctor Seeing a doctor in a clinic indicates an urgent need for help. If the dreamer meets the doctor at a social gathering, it is a sign of good health.

Dog This signifies that the dreamer has a desperate need for security in his relationships with others, and indicates his willingness to enjoy the protection provided by another person.

Dolphin The dreamer is seeking solutions to problems in the realm of magic and mysticism. It also suggests that the dreamer is removed from reality.

Dominoes Winning a game of dominoes indicates that the dreamer enjoys being appreciated by others and receiving compliments. Losing a game of dominoes means that the dreamer's problems also trouble others.

Donkey The braying of a donkey means that the dreamer is in a process of overcoming a painful family relationship. Leading a donkey by a rope attests to the strength of the dreamer's will power. If the dreamer is a child, it means he needs friends.

Door A closed door warns of wastefulness and extravagance. An open door, through which people can enter and leave, suggests that the dreamer will soon experience economic difficulties due to poor business management. A revolving door indicates surprises and new experiences.

Doorman Doorman (in a hotel or luxury building) signifies the dreamer's fierce longing to go on trips to other countries; alternatively, it shows the desire to make far-reaching changes in one's life.

Dough This is a symbol of wealth, money and property.

Dove This attests to a happy family life and great economic success. A flock of doves portends a journey or long trip.

Dragon A dragon means that in times of distress, the dreamer turns to a higher power for help, and does not himself make any effort on his own part to improve his situation. If

the dreamer is young, a dragon is a sign of an upcoming wedding.

Drinking Drinking alcoholic beverages indicates financial loss. If the dreamer sees himself drunk, he can expect great success. Drinking water, however, predicts being let down by someone close.

Driving If the dreamer is the driver, it means that he feels the need to act independently in life. If another person is driving, it is a sign that the dreamer trusts him. A dream about speeding intimates that the dreamer suffers from emotional problems.

Drowning If the dreamer sees himself drowning, it is a sign that cooperation with a professional colleague will be profitable. If the dreamer sees other people drowning, it foretells bad things in the future.

Duck This symbolizes happiness and good luck.

Dwarf This is an indication of good tidings. A sick or wounded dwarf suggests that the dreamer has hidden enemies.

Dying If the dreamer sees himself dying in a dream, it indicates a bad conscience or guilt feelings. If another person is dying, it means that the dreamer is trying to shake off feelings of responsibility for that person.

Eagle An eagle in a dream is not to be taken lightly. It is quite significant and indicates an extraordinary desire on the part of the dreamer to fulfill his potential.

Earth Earth symbolizes abundance and good things awaiting the dreamer. Arid land indicates disrespect of others and the need for soul-searching.

Eating This heralds confidence and economic stability. Eating together with another person signifies enduring friendship.

Eavesdropping If others are eavesdropping on the dreamer, it warns of trouble. If the dreamer is eavesdropping on others, he can expect happy surprises!

Edifice The meaning of the dream lies in the height of the edifice. Average height indicates changes in the near future. A higher-than-average edifice portends brilliant success in the near future.

Egg The appearance of an egg or the eating of an egg indicates that the dreamer will soon increase his wealth and become more established in life. A broken or rotten egg portends failure or loss.

Eggs Dreaming about a number of eggs means improvement in the dreamer's financial situation. Two eggs in a nest attests to the support of a loving family. Three eggs in a nest indicate an addition to the family!

Egg Yolk Good times are on the way. If a gambler dreams of the yolk of an egg, it means that he will have success at gambling.

Elbow This indicates that the dreamer is involved in activities that do not do justice to his abilities.

Elephant This predicts that the dreamer will meet people who will become his friends.

Elevator If the elevator is ascending, it means that the dreamer is yearning for positive changes in his life. A descending elevator indicates the absence of financial success and a lack of initiative.

Emptiness An empty container or a feeling of emptiness warns of a bitter disappointment that the dreamer will have to cope with and that will weaken him severely, both physically and mentally.

Engagement This foretells temporary disagreements with one's partner that will be resolved.

Envelope A sealed envelope indicates hardship, complexes, frustration and difficulties. An open envelope signifies that the dreamer will overcome obstacles that are not too formidable.

Envy/Jealousy
If the dreamer is envious of another person, it predicts possible disappointment. If another person is envious of the dreamer, it heralds success and good luck.

Eulogy
This is a sign of good news (usually marriage) brought by a close friend.

Eve and the Apple
Dreaming about the story of Eve in the Garden of Eden usually symbolizes the dreamer's ability to withstand temptation.

Evening
Dreaming of a pleasant evening predicts that the dreamer will soon enjoy a period of tranquillity and calm.

Explosion
This means that one of the dreamer's friends is in danger.

Eye Doctor
This warns the dreamer to keep his eyes open and be aware of his situation in order not to miss any opportunities that present themselves.

Eyeglasses/Binoculars
These indicate that the dreamer will experience a great improvement in his life, as things that were previously unclear to him will be clarified and understood.

Face Seeing his face in a mirror indicates to the dreamer that in the near future he will be privy to secrets that will influence his life significantly.

Failure Contrary to what might be expected, this actually predicts success and overcoming obstacles.

Fair/Bazaar Dreaming about being at a fair means that the dreamer must maintain a low profile in the near future and not be conspicuous.

Fame A dream about fame, whether that of the dreamer or of somebody close to him, warns of events that will be a source of nervousness and restlessness.

Fan An elaborate fan signifies that the dreamer is arrogant and egocentric. A new fan predicts good news. An old fan indicates that there is reason to be concerned about serious incidents or unpleasant news.

Farm/Ranch A walk around a farm means success in business. If the dreamer is in love, a happy relationship can be expected.

Farmer This suggests a life of prosperity and abundance; success in all areas: economic, social, personal and health.

Father When the dreamer is addressed by his father, joyful events will soon occur in his life. If the father merely appears in the dream, worries and problems can be expected.

Fatigue This warns against making incorrect decisions that the dreamer will regret all his life.

Faucet A faucet with water flowing out of it indicates business growth and financial success.

Fence Breaking down a fence in a dream is a sign that problems will be resolved in the near future. If a young woman dreams of a fence, it indicates that she is longing to be married and have children. A green fence signifies true love.

Fern This indicates an unusually strong sexual appetite.

Fever A high fever warns against wrongful actions and deeds which bring negative results.

Fig A fig is a prediction of good news.

Finger A hurt finger indicates a wounded self-image. The hurt finger of another person indicates incitement, vicious gossip or slander, all directed against the dreamer.

Fire This warns of problems that might arise in the vicinity of the dreamer.

Fireplace This is indicative of an upcoming period of prosperity, growth and economic stability for the dreamer.

Fish A single fish heralds success or means that the dreamer has a particularly successful and brilliant child. A school of fish means that the dreamer's friends care about him and are doing things for his benefit. Fishing in a dream signifies treachery on the part of a friend or friends. Eating fish predicts success following hard work.

Fish Eggs A sign of serenity and comfort for the dreamer.

Flag This means that the dreamer has a pleasant and tranquil character. Waving a flag in a contest means that the dreamer should take a break from the rat race and rest. A torn flag indicates disgrace.

Flash Flood This is an indication of danger on the horizon. Overcoming a flash flood or strong stream of water indicates overcoming obstacles and achieving success as a result of hard work.

Fleas Fleas mean that the dreamer's life is chaotic and extremely disorganized.

Floating Dreaming about floating in the air is very common. It usually indicates that the dreamer should focus his efforts on one objective.

Flood/Heavy Rain This symbolizes hardship and the inability to reach an understanding with one's surroundings.

Flowers Picking flowers in a dream signifies that the dreamer may count on his friends not to let him down. Throwing flowers in a dream is a prediction of a quarrel with someone close to him in the future. If the dream is about arranging flowers, a pleasant surprise can be expected.

Flute If the dreamer himself is playing the flute, it is an indication of hidden musical talent. Listening to the flute being played by somebody else means that the dreamer can rely on his friends.

Fly (insect) This indicates everyday worries and concerns.

Flying If the dreamer sees himself flying in the sky, it indicates that he does not have both feet firmly planted on the ground. He is not aware of his serious financial situation and ought to save more money and rethink his economic strategies.

Fog If the dreamer is in fog, it is a sign that his plans will be fulfilled. If fog is seen from afar, it indicates disagreement between the dreamer and those close to him.

Folder/Binder This means that the dreamer needs to consult with friends or receive assistance from them.

Food If the dreamer sees himself eating and enjoying himself, it heralds good and happy times to come: His aspirations will be realized!

Foot When a person's foot appears in a dream, it means

that the dreamer suffers from physical ailments which stem from his mind.

Forest Entering a dense forest suggests problems in the near future, particularly in the financial realm.

Fortress If the dreamer is inside a fortress, it means that he possesses a burning desire to become rich. If a fortress is seen in the distance, it suggests frustration and a feeling of having missed out. If the dreamer lives in the fortress, it means that the dreamer will acquire much wealth.

Fox This indicates that the dreamer is esteemed by those around him and enjoys a good reputation. If the dreamer chases a fox, it means that he is divorced from reality.

Friend If a friend appears in a dream, it means that he is in trouble or in danger.

Frogs These symbolize a good, happy and carefree life.

Fruit This is usually a prediction of good and pleasant things for the dreamer in the future.

Fruit (dried) A warning: The dreamer was not cautious when taking a certain stand, or he made a hasty decision.

Fuel/Gasoline A warning: The dreamer must distance himself from any situation which might lead to a confrontation with those close to him.

Fur Dry fur predicts wealth, good luck and happiness. Wet fur heralds success only after an about-face in one's life.

G

Gaiety A dream of especially great merriment, laughter and joy actually warns of hard times ahead.

Gaining Weight This predicts bad times for the dreamer in the near future.

Galloping Galloping on a horse confirms that the dreamer is on a direct path to success.

Gambling Actively gambling at a table in a dream symbolizes a future loss in business.

Game If the dreamer is participating in a competitive game, it means that he will soon receive good, happy news. If the dreamer is just watching a game, it means that in reality, he is very jealous of one of his friends.

Gang This reflects the dreamer's profound need for belonging and intimacy. A violent meeting with members of a gang suggests a fear of intimacy and close relationships.

Dream Interpretation

Garden Good tidings: a successful marriage, economic prosperity and material abundance. A garden with blooming flowers symbolizes an expanding business and inner peace. A vegetable garden indicates the need to take precautionary measures.

Garlic Dreaming of garlic is interpreted according to the dreamer's taste: If he likes garlic, it is a positive dream predicting success. If he is revolted by garlic, it portends bad times.

Gate A closed gate indicates social problems. A broken gate means problems on the ladder of promotion at work. If the dreamer sees himself swinging on the gate, it means that he prefers resting to working.

Gazelle This signifies that the dreamer is a loner.

Germ This is an indication of the dreamer's hypochondria and constant fear of illness.

Getting Lost This attests to frustration, embarrassment, confusion and a general dissatisfaction with life, especially regarding a romantic relationship in which the dreamer is involved.

Ghost The appearance of a ghost and a conversation with it indicate difficulties coping with someone's death and the desire to make contact with the world of the dead.

Giant This is a sign of the dreamer's ability to cope with and overcome problems, despite the hardships involved. It may also be an indication of an emotional problem that manifests itself mainly in feelings of inferiority.

Gift If the dreamer receives a gift from somebody, it means that the latter is plotting against him, attempting to deceive and undermine him.

Giraffe This signifies serious sexual problems, particularly if the dreamer is a single man.

Glory This is a sign that the dreamer has reached the peak of his achievements and from here on it is downhill all the way.

Gloves Losing gloves means a loss of control in business or a financial loss due to incorrect decision-making.

Glue This signifies confidence and a senior position in the workplace. If the dream is about fixing objects with glue, it is a warning about financial problems.

Goat This symbolizes virility. It sometimes foretells a substantial reward for hard work.

God If one dreams about God as an abstraction, as a concrete object (such as a religious sculpture) or as a deity image, or if one dreams of any kind of ritual, this reflects the dreamer's connection to religion. A dream of God heralds serenity, stability and security.

Gold Finding gold in a dream means that the dreamer will accomplish great things and attain the goals which he has set for himself. Losing gold means that the dreamer underestimates important issues. Touching gold means that the dreamer will take up a new hobby or occupation.

Goose A warning: The dreamer's expectations will not be fulfilled. If he dreams about killing a goose, great success can be expected.

Grapefruit This is an indication of health problems and a lack of energy and vitality.

Grapes These symbolize hedonism and the pursuit of pleasure.

Grass This indicates that whatever the dreamer desires is within his reach. There is no need for him to wander far off, as it is within his grasp. Green lawns indicate that wishes and expectations will be fulfilled.

Grasshopper A threat is hanging over the dreamer's head.

Grave Dreaming about a grave symbolizes everything the dreamer is lacking: health for a sick person, money for someone of limited means, marriage for single people, etc.

Grove If one dreams about a grove, particularly a green grove, it means that life will change for the better. A dying grove (as a result of fire or disease) means that the dreamer should make provision for his old age.

Guidance/Instruction

This means that in the near future there is likely to be an encounter with a person who has a positive influence over the dreamer.

Gun/Pistol Dreaming of a shot from a pistol suggests a lack of progress in business, as well as stagnation. The dreamer must change his ways in order to alter the trend.

Gutter (of a roof) The gutter in all its forms means that the dreamer can expect a long and worry-free life. Climbing up a gutter-pipe indicates that the dreamer wants to run away from solving his problems.

Gypsy A warning: The dreamer must watch out for a swindler who will make him suffer in the future. If the dreamer himself appears as a gypsy, it is a sign that in the future he will wander to another land to seek happiness.

Hair Thick, healthy hair means that the dreamer will soon be involved in successful projects. A dream about unusually colored hair indicates anxiety, hesitation and suspicion.

Hairdresser Dreaming about a hairdresser reflects the dreamer's dejection and depression.

Hammer The dreamer should consider his steps carefully and not waste money.

Hand A dirty hand means that the dreamer is facing a difficult period in his life. A bound hand indicates that his sadness will turn into happiness and joy.

Handcuffs These symbolize an impossible relationship or problems related to the judicial system. A dream of being released from handcuffs means that the dreamer is not an ordinary person.

Handicap If the dreamer dreams that he is handicapped, he can expect an improvement in his status and in other areas of life. Overcoming a handicap means that the dreamer will overcome obstacles along his path; the opposite is true as well.

Handkerchief Searching for a handkerchief in a dream is a sign of an imminent separation. If a handkerchief is found easily, it means that the dreamer will soon receive a gift.

Hanging If the dreamer sees himself being hanged, it indicates a promising career. If another person is being hanged, it means that one of the dreamer's acquaintances will become famous.

Happiness Contrary to what it seems, dreaming of happiness forecasts times of hardship and danger, particularly at the workplace.

Harp Hearing the sound of a harp attests to the dreamer's melancholy nature. A broken harp means that he has health problems. If he himself is playing the harp, it is a warning that he is a victim of some sort of deception connected to his love life.

Harvest One of the best images that can appear in a dream. It predicts economic, domestic and social success.

Hat If the dreamer wears a hat, it signifies imminent disappointment. If he loses a hat, it means he will soon receive a gift. Finding a hat in a dream is a sign that the dreamer will soon lose a small item. The inability to remove one's hat is a warning of disease.

Head If the dreamer sees himself wounded in the head, it is a sign that he has hidden enemies.

Headache This indicates that one of the dreamer's friends needs his help.

Headlights If the dreamer is blinded by the headlights of a car, it means that he should take steps quickly in order to prevent possible complications.

Heart Any type of dream about a heart heralds good tidings in all areas of life.

Heaviness A feeling of heaviness means that the dreamer is grappling with heavy and fateful issues.

Heel A broken heel means that the dreamer will have to confront problems and hardship in the near future.

Hell This indicates that the dreamer is greedy and materialistic, and what preoccupies him most is money. A dream about hell does not bode well. Financial losses can be expected, much to the joy of the dreamer's enemies.

Hen/Rooster A hen with chicks indicates the need to plan ahead with precision before acting.

Hearing a rooster in a dream indicates exaggerated self-confidence.

Heron This suggests a change occurring in the dreamer's life. Some interpret the heron as a symbol of stagnation, lack of development and being stuck in a rut.

Hiding-Place If the dreamer hides in a hiding-place, it is a sign that he will soon receive bad news.

Hippopotamus This warns of being overweight or refers to feelings of inferiority.

Honey This symbolizes happiness and joy. The dreamer will attain his objectives and enjoy the fruits of his labor and efforts.

Honor This is a sign that the dreamer must take precautions in money matters and adopt more economical patterns of behavior.

Horn (animal) Dreaming about an animal's horn signifies sexual problems. The interpretation of the dream depends on the context in which the horn appears.

Horse Dreaming about a horse symbolizes passion or lust; riding a white horse – business and social success; riding a black horse – failure; a runaway horse – financial losses; falling off a horse – a hasty, rushed marriage; riding a wild horse – strong sexual passion.

Horse-Race If the dreamer is a woman, it indicates imminent marital problems. If the dreamer is a man, it warns of danger from an unexpected source. The dreamer must take care and beware. (See also Horse.)

Horseshoe This means that the dreamer will embark on a sea voyage in the near future.

Hospital If a healthy person dreams about a hospital, it means that he fears disease and death. Dreaming about being treated in a hospital by a medical staff indicates fear of the future.

Hotel This means that the dreamer is in need of changes in his life. It also warns against making hasty decisions.

Hot Pepper This reflects feelings of pride resulting from the success of someone close to the dreamer.

Hugging Hugging, particularly a family member or a person close to the dreamer, reflects his need to give of himself to others.

Hunchback This indicates imminent success.

1

Ice-Skating This has two meanings in a dream: It warns of flattery, or of an unstable relationship with the person whom the dreamer loves most.

Insect (crawling) Despite unpleasant connotations, a significant, positive change can be expected in the dreamer's life.

Insect This symbolizes difficulties and disappointments in the business or family life of the dreamer.

Insult This indicates that the dreamer yearns for change in his life (in his job or place of residence).

Intersection This signifies exactly that: The dreamer has come to a crossroad in his life and must make decisions that will affect his destiny.

Interview An interview suggests that there will soon be a promotion and good news from a close acquaintance.

Ironing This is a sign of a good period during which the dreamer will cooperate successfully with those around him.

Ivy This indicates that the dreamer is sensitive and dedicated to the traditions he grew up with and to the people close to him.

Jasmine This indicates that the dreamer is not exploiting even a fraction of his talents and abilities.

Jewelry This is a sign that that the dreamer is lucky. Broken jewelry portends disappointment. Receiving jewelry as a gift signifies a happy marriage. Losing jewelry in a dream suggests troubles caused by gambling.

Journey This means that the dreamer may expect changes in his life.

Judge This clearly indicates that the dreamer must not be quick to judge other people or determine their guilt or innocence.

Jug A jug is a symbol of good luck. If the jug is full, this is extremely good luck.

Jumping Jumping in a dream is not a good sign: it means the dreamer can expect hardships, disappointment or frustration.

Kangaroo This means the dreamer is not satisfied with one partner.

Kennel/Doghouse This indicates emotional stress and a lack of serenity. It warns of health problems and physical weakness.

Kettle If the kettle has boiled, it warns against loss of assets. If the water has not yet boiled, it predicts success and good luck.

Key Any situation involving a key (except the loss of a key) is good news: success in one's personal, social, financial and family life. The loss of a key is a warning of things to come.

King If a king appears or speaks to the dreamer, it means good things or a change for the better in the dreamer's life.

Kiss If the dreamer is kissing a stranger, it is a sign that he is not completely aware of what is going on around him, and this could do him great harm.

Kitchen This appears mainly in women's dreams. It attests to satisfaction with family life and loyal friends.

Kite Flying a kite in a dream indicates that the dreamer enjoys sharing his feelings with others and that he will attain all of his objectives in life.

Knee A healthy knee signifies success and happiness. An injured knee indicates a need to deal with difficulties that will put the dreamer's patience to the test.

Knife Dreaming about a knife is usually a warning. Any type of knife can only mean bad times: domestic quarrels, lack of understanding, violent outbursts and fears.

Knight Dreaming about a knight indicates that the dreamer is bothered by issues of status and hierarchy, as well as the relationship between the ruler and the ruled.

Knitting A dream about knitting anything is a sign of a good life. If the knitting needle or the ball of wool falls down, it warns of enemies.

Knot Any knot in a dream is a sign of economic problems and financial losses.

Dream Interpretation

Label If a label or sticker indicating a name or an item appears, it heralds a future full of surprises.

Ladder If the dreamer climbs a ladder without mishap, it is a sign that his ambitions are about to be realized. Fear of ascending a ladder, or an accident (such as falling off the ladder) is a dire prediction. A ladder leaning against a wall means that one of the dreamer's relatives is disloyal to him.

Ladybug If this red insect with the black dots appears, it is a sign that the dreamer will soon chance upon a golden opportunity which will allow him to fulfill his greatest dreams.

Lake The dreamer is soon to enjoy the fruits of his past labors. Positive developments in his life can be expected.

Lamp/Flashlight A bright lamp means that the dreamer is a honest person and seeks justice. A dim lamp indicates a feeling of embarrassment and confusion.

Landing (from flight) This predicts hardships for the dreamer in the near future. However, he will overcome them.

Lark This is a sign of joyous events and a perfect marriage for the dreamer.

Lateness If the dreamer is late, despite his attempts to arrive on time, it attests to the fact that people value his opinion and are waiting to hear what he has to say.

Laughter The dreamer's laughter is actually an indication of sad things that he is liable to experience. If others are laughing, it is a sign that the dreamer's life will be happy and full of joy.

Laundry A warning: Failure and domestic problems will arise soon.

Laurels This is a rare image symbolizing forthcoming honor, glory and fame in the dreamer's life.

Law All the elements relating to the law (including courts, police, lawyers, etc.) give the dreamer a warning: Think carefully before making a decision concerning financial issues.

Lawsuit This means that the dreamer has a conservative nature: He lives a full and serene life, but is not spontaneous and does not break his routine easily.

Lawyer This means that the dreamer is in need of assistance, advice and guidance.

Leaves If one dreams about a tree with green leaves, it is a sign that one's love life will improve. Withered leaves mean that the dreamer is frustrated with a bad decision he made.

Lecture If the dreamer is giving a lecture in front of an audience, it indicates that he will enjoy great professional success.

Leg If the dreamer's legs are emphasized, it means that he is rational, self-aware, and has a lot of self-confidence.

Legumes These symbolize economic success and prosperity in business.

Lemon This signifies despair resulting from a great love for and disappointment in one's partner.

Leopard A warning: An enemy is attempting to harm the dreamer and may succeed.

Letter Writing or receiving a letter in a dream means that unexpected good news is on its way.

Lettuce This is an indication of problems relating to sexuality and a person's love life in general.

Lice These signify that the dreamer suffers from feelings of social alienation or inferiority.

Lie If the dreamer or another person lies in a dream, it is a warning to beware of a shady deal or fraud.

Light The meaning of the dream changes according to the intensity of the light. A bright, shining light – wealth and happiness; a dull light – disappointment and depression; a green light – the dreamer's jealousy.

Lightning This dream heralds particularly good tidings, especially concerning agriculture and farming.

Lily The lily is considered a symbol of holiness amongst Christians and is connected to holy sites and people.

Limping If the dreamer is limping, it is a sign that he will always have friends around him. If another person is limping, it is a sign that the dreamer is about to be bitterly disappointed.

Line If the dreamer is standing on line, this indicates that a relationship with an old friend, severed due to an argument, will be soon renewed.

Lion This is a sign that one of the dreamer's friends will be very successful; in the future, the dreamer will benefit highly from this success and will receive help from the friend.

Lips Fleshy lips signify happiness and joy for the dreamer. Thin, pale lips are an indication of anguish and pain.

Lizard This is a warning that a person with bad intentions is conspiring against the dreamer, and he should be careful.

Loan If someone requests a loan from the dreamer, it means that the latter will soon suffer considerable financial losses. If the dreamer is unsuccessful in his attempt to pay back a loan, it is a good sign, foretelling an improvement in his economic situation.

Dream Interpretation

Loss Losses, wounds or injuries are interpreted as warning signs. Be alert to and aware of changes in life or to any situation fraught with potential danger.

Love If an unmarried person dreams of love, it indicates marriage in the near future. If the dreamer is married, it predicts a domestic quarrel. A dream about a couple's relationship in general – one that is based on pure intentions – hints at happiness, joy and success. If the dream relationship is based on exploitation, it symbolizes disappointment in reality.

M

Machines Machines used for production or other sophisticated machinery indicate complex problems in all areas of life.

Madness A dream about madness of any kind is actually a sign of particularly good luck, predicting happiness, prosperity and success.

Magic This predicts changes for the better in the dreamer's life, especially in finance and health.

Man/Woman Dreaming about a man indicates good things. Dreaming about a woman represents a warning to think carefully before making an important or fateful decision.

Manager/Boss Any dream about a manager or boss, whether the dreamer himself is the manager or another person is the boss, indicates a promotion at work, as well as improvement in economic and social status.

Mansion If the dreamer enters a mansion, he can expect good news. If he leaves a mansion in a hurry, it predicts serious problems that await him.

Map This is a sign that the dreamer can expect some kind of change in his life.

Marching Marching along an uneven road suggests misunderstandings and a lack of communication with the dreamer's surroundings.

Marriage/Nuptials Dreaming about marriage, particularly if the groom is elegantly dressed, is a sign of a great disappointment that awaits the dreamer, or of a significant decrease in his status.

Mask This signifies that the dreamer is two-faced. It also warns him of betrayal by a person close to him who is acting behind his back in an attempt to undermine him.

Meat If the dreamer cooks, it means good tidings. If he eats meat prepared by someone else, he can expect bad times.

Medicine Any kind of medicine in a dream signifies that in the near future, the dreamer's life will be temporarily upset by worries and hardships.

Medium (clairvoyant) Dreams about an individual who acts as an intermediary between the world of the living and the world of the dead predict that the dreamer will undergo a serious crisis in the near future.

Melon This means that the dreamer can expect changes for the better in his life.

Mermaid Dreaming about something that does not exist in reality signifies the search for impossible love.

Milk Purchasing milk portends good times; selling milk – success and good luck; boiling milk – success following great effort; sour and spoiled milk – domestic problems.

Millstone This represents hard work for which there is not sufficient remuneration.

Mint (plant) Dreaming about mint means good news: the dreamer will soon receive a substantial inheritance from an unexpected source.

Mole This is a warning of danger hovering over the dreamer's head.

Money Finding money is a sign of a unique opportunity that was missed. Winning money means that the dreamer should consider his actions carefully. Stealing money indicates a fear of losing authority.

Monk/Nun This indicates that the dreamer's problems or troubles will soon be resolved and that the dreamer will enjoy a period of tranquillity and serenity.

Monkey This means that the dreamer has a dishonest relationship with a close acquaintance.

Monster A monster appearing in different forms in a dream signifies that the dreamer suffers from extreme fear to the point of paralysis.

Moon This symbolizes outstanding success in love.

Mosquito This is a sign that enemies are plotting evil against the dreamer.

Moth A relationship with someone close with the dreamer will become strained.

Mother The nature of the relationship between the dreamer and his mother is of the utmost importance. Usually, dreaming about a mother speaks of pregnancy in the near future. However, it may also symbolize strong friendship, honesty, wisdom, generosity and a successful married life.

Mother-in-law If the dreamer argues with his mother-in-law, it means that he wants peace at home.

Motor This symbolizes the desire to be a leader and to be at the center of things.

Mountain If the ascent is very difficult, it portends encounters with obstacles that the dreamer will struggle to overcome. An easy, fast ascent means that the dreamer possesses the ability to cope with crises successfully. If he meets other people during the climb, it signifies that the dreamer will have to seek help from others on his path to success.

Mourning This symbolizes loss, sorrow and pain.

Mouse This warns of potential harm to the dreamer as a result of unnecessary interference by others in his life.

Mouth A big mouth means great future wealth. A small mouth means financial problems.

Mud Dreaming about mud symbolizes dissatisfaction.

Dream Interpretation

Extricating oneself from mud or quicksand represents the ability to get out of difficult and complex situations.

Mushrooms These signify that the dreamer will soon forge significant social bonds.

Music Harmonious and pleasant music symbolizes success and a good life. Discordant and cacophonous sounds signal disruptions during a journey or long trip.

Mustard A warning: Beware of taking bad advice.

Mute/Dumb This indicates that the dreamer must keep a secret, or else he will suffer harm.

Nails (finger) Long nails mean happiness with one's spouse and success in business. Short nails warn of financial losses.

Nakedness Walking or swimming naked and alone means that one's spouse is very loyal. Walking naked among clothed people predicts a period full of scandal.

Name If the dreamer hears someone calling his name, it is a sign that he will soon require help from someone close to him.

Narrow Passage A feeling of suffocation and a lack of air while dreaming of being in a narrow passage signifies the dreamer's very strong sexual passion or feelings of pressure and anxiety.

Neck A dream about receiving a compliment about one's neck signifies that one has a full love life.

Necklace This symbolizes the dreamer's desire to be at the center of things. Losing a necklace indicates hard times in the near future.

Needle Finding a needle in a dream predicts a strong friendship with a new acquaintance. Threading a needle symbolizes the dreamer's responsible nature. A broken needle is a sign of acceptance and reconciliation. Sewing means that the dreamer suffers from loneliness.

Nervousness Good news is on the way!

News Strangely, good news in a dream warns of problems and worries. Bad news, however, heralds good luck and success in the near future.

Newspaper This means that the dreamer's reputation is being compromised.

Night Darkness and night symbolize a lack of mental clarity, as well as confusion and a lack of clarity in the dreamer's life.

Nightingale The nightingale sparks an immediate association with melody and pleasant sounds. It means that romance will dominate the dreamer's life for a short while.

Noise If there is a lot of noise around the dreamer, it means that he will play the role of arbiter and peacemaker in a quarrel between two people close to him.

Dream Interpretation

Nomad If the dreamer or another person appears as a nomad or a wanderer, he has a burning desire for change in his life.

Nose If the dreamer sees himself with a large nose in a dream, it indicates great wealth and economic prosperity. A small nose means that one of the dreamer's immediate family members or relatives will disgrace the family.

Note If the dreamer receives a note, it means that although he requires his friends' help, they will not offer it.

Notebook The dreamer has problems breaking away from his past.

Nurse If a nurse appears in a dream, it suggests good things to come – mainly success at work or an improvement in one's economic situation.

Oak The oak tree is a symbol of health and a good quality of life.

Oats A horse eating oats indicates that the dreamer has unfinished tasks at hand.

Ocean This signifies a desire for a new beginning, or for withdrawal and inner contemplation. A calm sea and a clear horizon represent a rosy future; a stormy sea predicts imminent danger.

Office If the dreamer works in an office, financial problems are predicted. Managing an office symbolizes ambitiousness and the ability to overcome obstacles.

Officer This indicates that the dreamer needs an authoritative figure in his life to map a path for him.

Oil A man's dream about oil represents a warning against difficult times, fraught with disappointments and frustration. If a woman dreams about oil, she will be respected and have a happy marriage.

Olive The olive symbolizes happiness and wealth for the dreamer. A dream about harvesting olives or about black olives predicts a birth in the family.

Onion This is an indication of difficulties, economic concerns, fear of losses. Peeling an onion symbolizes renewed efforts to try and achieve a coveted objective.

Opera A dream of an opera that is unpleasant to the dreamer's ears is a sign of crisis and failure, conflict and inner turmoil. If the dreamer participates in an opera, it symbolizes a desire to reveal a hidden talent that has not yet come to the fore.

Opponent/Rival A dream about an opponent is a sign that the dreamer's wishes will soon come true.

Orange Eating or seeing an orange in a dream suggests a significant improvement in one's lifestyle.

Orchard If the orchard is surrounded by a fence, it means that the dreamer yearns for something unattainable.

Dream Interpretation

Orchestra Listening to an orchestra playing music indicates that the dreamer will be very famous. A dream about playing in an orchestra predicts a significant promotion at work.

Orchid This attests to the dreamer's strong sexual desires.

Orphanhood If the dreamer or another person is orphaned, it means that a new and positive personality will enter the dreamer's life, constituting a highly dominant force.

Ostrich This is a sign that the dreamer or a family member has health problems.

Oven The dreamer is in need of warm and loving human contact.

Owl This symbolizes sad things: melancholy, pain, loss, etc.

Package

Receiving a package means that there are positive changes in store for the dreamer or for those close to him.

Packing This indicates a yearning for change. If the dreamer does not finish packing, it is a sign of frustration.

Pain This shows that the dreamer is surrounded by a supportive and loving environment. The stronger the pain, the more significant the dreamer is to those around him.

Painting This indicates that something the dreamer has long been wishing for will come true.

Palace If the dreamer finds himself in a palace or great hall, it is a sign of unexpected problems. If he did not see the entrance to this place, it means that good news regarding romance is coming his way.

Palms (of the hands) If the hands are far from the body, it shows that the dreamer and those around him do not understand each other. Hairy palms the dreamer has a wild imagination; dirty palms jealousy; folded hands emotional stress; bound hands the dreamer is very restrained.

Paper (sheets) Sheets of paper signify restlessness and a lack of clarity. The cleaner and lighter the sheets, the greater the chance of extricating oneself from the problematic situation and turning over a new leaf.

Paradise This indicates a change for the better in life. The transition will manifest itself in a move from preoccupation with the material world to preoccupation with the spiritual world.

Parents Parent-child relationships indicate various family problems (not necessarily with parents).

Parrot A parrot which is tied up suggests that the dreamer enjoys gossiping or is a victim of gossip.

Peach Opportunities to enjoy pleasurable experiences can be expected in the future.

Peacock This warns against conceit and excessive pride.

Peanuts These signify that the dreamer is sociable and will be blessed with many friends.

Pear This indicates that others are gossiping and talking about the dreamer, his friends or relatives behind his back.

Peas These herald a good period of prosperity and economic growth.

Peddler This predicts financial success occurring in an unusual manner.

Pen If the dreamer is writing with a pen, he will hear from a person with whom he has been out of touch for a long time.

Penguin This signifies that the dreamer has an adventurous character and aspires to go on journeys.

Penis Dreaming about a penis has a sexual interpretation which depends on the character of the dreamer.

Perfume A dream about perfume is a sign of good news, particularly concerning love relationships.

Pestering/Bothering Any kind of pestering means that nonsense, useless chatter and small talk are liable to cause harm.

Dream Interpretation

Pheasant This is a symbol of wealth, well-being and economic prosperity.

Photography Any sort of photography indicates a long journey. If a woman dreams about a camera, it means that she will soon have a heart-warming meeting with a man.

Picture This shows a strong desire to succeed and avoid failure.

Pig In Western culture, a pig symbolizes a difficult personality, one that does not get on well with others. In the Far East, it is a sign of economic abundance.

Pillow This is a warning against an inappropriate action by the dreamer that may cause concern, embarrassment and a lack of confidence.

Pills If the dreamer sees pills in a package or a bottle, it means that he will soon embark on a journey or a trip.

Pineapple This is an indication of days of happiness and joy, especially in the company of close friends.

Pine Cone A closed pine cone symbolizes a tight-knit family; an open pine cone indicates a family that has separated and drifted apart.

Pleasure Boat This indicates that the dreamer longs to go on a vacation and let his hair down.

Plum This is a clear sign that the dreamer has enemies of whom he is not aware.

Pocket A pocket symbolizes the womb. The dream is interpreted according to the context in which the pocket appeared. It may indicate the dreamer's desire to return to the womb, or, alternatively, his desire to storm back into life.

Police A dream involving the police on any level means that the dreamer will soon receive assistance which will extricate him from the crisis he is now going through. A dream about confrontation with a policeman or about arrest shows that the dreamer suffers from confusion and guilt.

Pomegranate A pomegranate or pomegranate tree suggests that the dreamer fears sexual infidelity on the part of his partner.

Porch If the dreamer stands on a porch, it means that day-to-day worries are bothering him.

Port/Harbor This symbolizes worries, conflicts with others, dissatisfaction and a lack of serenity.

Postman This is a sign that the dreamer is worried about financial, business-related or social difficulties.

Post Office Dreaming of a post office indicates that the dreamer has a guilty conscience concerning an outstanding debt or commitment.

Potato This symbolizes calm, stability and satisfaction with one's life.

Potsherds These portend a period of happiness and joy, as well as of economic prosperity.

Prayer If the dreamer is praying, it is a sign that a good period, filled with happiness and joy, is approaching. If prayer takes place without the dreamer, it is a sign that the dreamer's deeds are harmful to others.

Pregnancy This is an indication of dissatisfaction with the dreamer's present situation and the longing to turn over a new leaf.

Prince/Princess This indicates that the dreamer possesses the hidden ability to fulfill his urgent need to improve his social status.

Prison about imprisonment warns about a change for the worse in physical health. A dream about an unsuccessful attempt to escape from prison is an indication of an obstacle in one's life that must be overcome. A dream about a successful escape from prison suggests success and the fulfillment of hopes.

Prize Winning a prize signifies the opposite: Heavy financial losses can be expected.

Procession/Parade A festive procession or parade indicate changes that will usher in a period of stormy events.

Profit If the dreamer receives a large sum of money, this is a sign of deception, denial and being led astray by one of his close friends.

Punch If the dreamer has punched someone, he should expect to lose a court case. If the dreamer has been punched, he should expect to win.

Dream Interpretation

Quarrel If the dreamer is involved in a quarrel, it means that someone is fiercely jealous of him. Alternatively, he will be lucky.

Queen This indicates that the dreamer will soon receive help or assistance from those close to him.

Quicksand If the dreamer is trapped in quicksand, it is a sign that his social and economic status is improving. If he sees another person trapped in quicksand, it is a sign that others will stand in the way of his attempts to achieve his objectives.

Quitting (a job)/Resignation
Dreaming about quitting a job, especially if the dreamer has a senior position, indicates that his plans will be realized in the near future.

Rabbit If the rabbit is white, it means that the dreamer is sexually unfulfilled and is dissatisfied with his sex life.

Rain This does not bode well. Gentle, light rain indicates that the dreamer will have to face disappointment and frustration; heavy, pounding rain means that the dreamer will have to cope with situations that will cause him despondency and depression.

Rainbow This is always a good sign: Happiness, joy, serenity and pleasure will come the dreamer's way.

Raisins These symbolize wastefulness and extravagance that need to be curbed.

Rake (the tool) This is an indication of great effort and hard work that must be expected on the road to glory.

Rape If a woman dreams of rape, it indicates a warped relationship with her partner.

Raspberry This symbolizes a strong desire for passionate sexual relations.

Rat This is a sign that a person very close to the dreamer is conspiring against him. If a pack of rats appears, it means that the dreamer's health is very poor.

Dream Interpretation

Raven This signifies mystical beliefs or black magic.

Recipe Dreaming about a recipe book indicates that the dreamer is blessed with good physical and mental health.

Recitation Learning a text by heart is a sign of problems that the dreamer must face and that he will overcome. This dream is a sign of the extraordinary success the dreamer will enjoy on any path that he might choose.

Reconciliation If the dreamer effects a reconciliation with a person with whom he has fought and severed relations, it suggests good tidings.

Religion Dreaming of a religious event signifies a positive and successful future: the dreamer will enjoy good times.

Religious Functionary The appearance of a religious functionary indicates hard times filled with problems, disappointments, anxiety and frustration.

Reptiles Any kind of reptile is usually a sign of conflicts or obstacles awaiting the dreamer.

Rescue If the dreamer is rescued in his dream, it indicates that he was misled or mistaken, and warns against making any momentous decisions.

Restaurant This usually symbolizes love and romance, but may also indicate that the dreamer lacks a warm family relationship. In addition, it may symbolize hedonism and love of the good life.

Revenge Any sort of revenge in a dream signifies that

Dream Interpretation

the dreamer will be guilty of causing a quarrel.

Rhinoceros This signifies a longing for male potency, as a result of sexual problems.

Ribbon This is a sign of extravagance. Dreaming about a bride wearing ribbons indicates that the groom's intentions are not honorable.

Rice Good things can be expected in one's personal or family life: an improvement in one's sex life, finding the perfect partner or domestic harmony.

Riot/Tumult Displays of violence, rage or wild behavior indicate that the dreamer's conscience is not clear, and that he is advised to reevaluate his actions carefully.

River If the dreamer is sitting on the bank of a river whose waters are clear, he will soon travel or go on a long trip. A stormy river with muddy water indicates obstacles on his path to success.

Road Dreaming about a difficult road, winding and full of potholes, is a sign of success in the personal and business realms. A smooth, straight road indicates family quarrels.

Roadblock This predicts a good period in life. The dreamer can expect a promotion at work and will succeed in attaining his objectives.

Robbery/Theft This is an indication of fears and anxieties stemming from economic difficulties.

Robin Dreaming about this bird is usually connected to its red color – the color of sex and love – or suggests an attempt to make amends with a person one loves.

Dream Interpretation

Rock This symbolizes danger and difficulties. The larger the rock, the greater the danger.

Rocking-Chair An empty rocking-chair is a sign that sadness and pain are coming the way of the dreamer as a result of separation from a loved one. Someone sitting in a rocking-chair is a sign of material and economic stability, as well as personal happiness.

Roller-Skates If the dreamer is roller-skating, it is a warning: He may be involved in an accident in the near future, and he should be careful.

Roof If a roof or the construction of a roof appears in a dream, it shows progress in one's life. Climbing onto a roof is a sign that one's ambitions will be fulfilled. Climbing quickly on to a roof indicates that success will arrive even more quickly. A penthouse apartment indicates success and prosperity.

Room (a closed room) This symbolizes the dreamer's repressed fears, or his unsatisfactory relationship with his partner.

Rope If the dreamer sees himself tied up with a rope, it is a sign that he has broken (or is about to break) a promise to a friend or betray a confidence. Climbing a rope suggests difficulties on the road to success. Tying a rope is an indication of the need to control others.

Roses These are a symbol of prosperity and success in all areas of life, particularly romance.

Rudeness If the dreamer is rude to someone in his dream, it shows that the dream concerns his relationship with his partner.

Ruler (for drawing lines) This indicates the dreamer's need to be objective and honest when judging others, although in reality, this is not possible.

Running This is a sign that during a trip in the near future, the dreamer will meet someone who will have a profound influence on his life.

Running Away/Fleeing If the dreamer is running away from something, it means that a close friend is conspiring against him and joining forces with his enemies. If a person who is close to the dreamer is running away, it signifies that the dreamer's family will soon increase in size. An unsuccessful attempt to run away indicates that certain problems have not been solved.

Rust
This symbolizes disappointment in the realm of romance.

S

Saddle This predicts travel or a trip accompanied by a surprise.

Sadness A feeling of sadness and even depression actually means the exact opposite: The dreamer may expect a period filled with happiness and joy in the near future.

Safe (deposit box)

This symbolizes marriage. Breaking into a safe predicts that the dreamer will marry someone he has not yet met. An empty safe means an early marriage. A full safe indicates a late marriage.

Sage (the herb) Dreaming about sage symbolizes the recovery from a serious disease, whether it is the dreamer's illness or that of someone close to him.

Sailing This is symbolic of a good future and a variety of opportunities open to the dreamer.

Sailor Dreaming about a sailor or seaman indicates sexual infidelity.

Saint This indicates that the dreamer relies on a higher power for help.

Salad Dreaming of preparing or eating a salad indicates that one of the dreamer's hidden talents will soon manifest itself and cover him with glory.

Salary If a person dreams of receiving a raise, it is a warning about an upcoming incident.

Salmon This symbolizes an obstacle that the dreamer will encounter, but one that he will eventually overcome through will power.

Salt This is a very positive dream which heralds good luck and success in all areas of life.

Sand This indicates conflicts and quarrels with family members.

Saw If a male dreamer dreams that he is sawing something, it is a sign that he is reliable. If a woman saws something in a dream, it means that one of her friends will soon offer her helpful advice.

Scaffolding This is a sign that an incorrect step taken by the dreamer may cause a lover's quarrel and even a break-up.

Scale (measuring) This indicates an aspiration for justice and the ability to judge properly. Occasionally, a scale appearing in a dream suggests conjugal conflict.

Scar This indicates the inability of the dreamer to break away from his past.

Scarf Dreaming about a scarf is not a good sign. If the dreamer sees himself wrapped in a scarf, it means that he has a tendency toward depression. If a woman dreams about a scarf that bothers her when she wears it, it means that an intimate secret concerning her life will soon be revealed.

Dream Interpretation

School Dreaming about school indicates anxiety about failure. If the dreamer is an adult, the dream indicates frustration and a feeling of missed opportunities and failure. If the dreamer is a young person, it means that he is avoiding responsibility.

Scissors A person close to the dreamer is pretending to be his friend; however, he is not.

Scratch If the dreamer scratches another person, it is a sign that he has a very critical nature.

Scratching This symbolizes unfounded concerns.

Screen This indicates that the dreamer suffers from emotional problems.

Seagull The seagull is a sign of bad news: the dreamer is likely to hear news that will cause him sadness and distress.

Search Searching for something warns that the dreamer is acting in haste, not paying attention to important and meaningful details. The search for a person signifies fear of loss.

Seeds (to plant) This means that the dreamer's elaborate plans for the future will indeed be realized.

Seeds A dream about any kind of seed always signifies good things. The dreamer will find happiness and blessings through his efforts.

Selling A dream about selling one's private property is a sign that the dreamer will have financial difficulties in the near future.

Dream Interpretation

Separation This means that the dreamer will have to make concessions in his life.

Servant If the dreamer has a servant in the dream, it means that his standard of living will increase and he will be financially successful.

Sewage Sewage in a dream is indicative of an unsuccessful marriage, of hidden enemies or of a bad business connection.

Shadows Dreaming of shadows indicates that there will be a great improvement in economic status as well as significant monetary profits.

Shampooing (the hair) This is an indication of gossip and revealed secrets.

Shark This signifies that the dreamer unconsciously fears the dark.

Sheep These show that it will be worthwhile for the dreamer to stick to his chosen path tenaciously.

Shell/Oyster This means that good and positive things are on their way: happiness, joy, financial and business success.

Shelter Searching for a shelter means that the dreamer is very fearful of enemies. Building a shelter signifies the desire to escape from one's enemies.

Shelves Empty shelves indicate that there will be losses and failures. Full shelves are a sign of great financial and material success.

Shepherd This symbolizes the dreamer's hidden need to be involved in spiritual matters.

Ship Dreaming about a ship is only meaningful if the ship's captain appears in the dream. If so, it indicates success in most areas of the dreamer's life.

Shooting If someone shoots the dreamer, it means that he fears significant losses in the future.

Short (physique) If the dreamer or one of his friends appears as a short person, it means that the dreamer will make progress in most areas of his life.

Shortage/Hunger This predicts particularly good things and indicates a positive turnabout in the dreamer's life.

Shovel Stoking a fire with a shovel indicates that the dreamer can expect good times.

Shower This symbolizes the desire for sexuality and love. A dream about taking a shower with a partner indicates a good sex life.

Sigh A dream in which the dreamer sighs is indicative of a good period, and means that the dreamer does not owe anyone anything.

Silk If a woman dreams about silk, it means that she is happy with her family and love life. If the dreamer is a man, it is a sign that he will be highly successful in business.

Silverware This represents a marriage in the family or of a close friend of the dreamer.

Singing If the dreamer or another person is singing, it

is a prediction of a difficult period, full of obstacles and problems.

Skeleton This is a sign that the dreamer's problems will all be solved soon.

Skin If a dreamer sees his skin, it indicates a non-spiritual, materialistic personality.

Skull This is a symbol of domestic problems.

Sky This indicates a change for the better, accompanied by happiness and joy.

Sleep If the dreamer sees himself sleeping, it warns of others who aim to harm him.

Smoke Black smoke warns of possible problems in family life.

Smoking This predicts an unfavorable period accompanied by frustration and anxiety.

Snail This heralds good, joyous news, particularly news that is very touching.

Snake A snake is a warning against falsehood. If someone dreams about a snake bite, it means that someone close to him is lying to him and deceiving him. Killing a snake in a dream indicates the end of a friendship.

Snow Any type of snow in a dream indicates extreme fatigue.

Soldier This indicates that the dreamer is involved in conflicts or quarrels.

Son/Daughter This represents the need for respect from others. A dream about a lost or sick son is a warning about the future.

Spider In the context of European culture, the spider symbolizes a woman. The dream means that a woman will control the dreamer's life (even if the dreamer is a woman).

Spider-Web A spider-web being woven around the dreamer means that the dreamer will achieve his objectives despite obstacles along the way.

Spools of Thread These indicate unhappy feelings due to the dreamer's inability to cope with the tasks at hand.

Spoon/Teaspoon Attests to a good and happy family life. Losing a spoon or teaspoon represents the dreamer's feeling that others are suspicious of him although he has done them no wrong.

Spy If the dreamer sees himself as a spy, it predicts an unsuccessful adventure.

Squirrel This predicts good times accompanied by success in all areas of life.

Stains These indicate difficulties, frustrations and fears.

Statue A statue is a sign of a self-imposed change in the dreamer's life.

Steer (animal) This indicates the dreamer's honesty and fairness, which are his most outstanding character traits. If more than one steer appears in a dream, it shows that this is the right time to take risks (A steer, as opposed to a bull or cow, is characterized by his horns; see Bull.)

Store/Shop If the dreamer is actually a storekeeper, it indicates business problems. If the dreamer does not own a shop, and he dreams that he is walking amongst the products on sale, it is a sign that he can expect good, pleasure-filled times.

Storeroom A tidy storeroom is a sign of economic prosperity, pleasure and abundance. An empty storeroom is a warning against incorrect decisions, especially in the monetary sphere.

Stork This symbolizes renewal and a change for the better in the dreamer's life.

Stranger Dreaming about a stranger, especially one wearing a black suit, represents a warning about a bad period and depression in the life of the dreamer.

Straw This reflects the dreamer's bad feelings. He sees his end and his destruction.

Struggle Triumph over another person in a struggle is a sign that the dreamer will overcome difficulties that stand in his way.

Suffering Contrary to what might be expected, dreaming about pain or suffering is actually an indication of happiness, joy and laughter coming the way of the dreamer in the near future.

Suffocating/Choking This expresses aggression and fear. If the dreamer is suffocating another person, it means that he feels hatred towards him. If the dreamer is being suffocated by another, it means that he deeply fears the person who is suffocating him in the dream.

Sugar This symbolizes a good period in the dreamer's life accompanied by feelings of wholeness and harmony with his environment.

Suicide This indicates the dreamer's desire to extricate himself from a difficult situation.

Suitcase If the suitcase belongs to the dreamer, it indicates that he will soon have to deal with problems. If the suitcase belongs to someone else, it means that he will soon embark on a trip.

Sums (addition) An incorrect sum warns against unsuccessful commercial negotiations.

Sunflower This signifies sunshine, light and warmth.

Swan This indicates a good family life. A black swan symbolizes a good and generous spouse; a white swan indicates a happy marriage and successful progeny.

Sweetness A dream about eating something sweet means that the dreamer possesses a high level of inner awareness and self-control.

Swimming If the dreamer sees himself swimming, it is a warning against taking unnecessary risks or gambling which will bring about significant losses.

Table This symbolizes a person's accomplishments in life. A set table signifies a comfortable family life. A work table, operating table, desk, etc., are interpreted according to the context of their appearance in the dream.

Tailor This is a sign that the dreamer is indecisive and easily influenced by others.

Tar Tar on a road signifies good health. Tar on the soles of shoes or floating in water means that the dreamer will soon embark on a trip. Boiling tar means personal problems.

Taxi If the dreamer sees himself hailing a taxi which then drives past him without stopping, it is a warning against being naive. If the dreamer hails a taxi uneventfully, he can expect a letter with good news in the near future.

Tea This suggests that the dreamer could be more resolute in his opinions and more decisive in his manner.

Teacher This indicates that the dreamer must examine his financial and social situation and act cautiously.

Tear A tear indicates extreme emotional changes.

Tears If tears are shed in a dream, it means that the dreamer will enjoy a rosy future and happy events.

Teeth Dreaming about teeth or about a dentist warns of health problems. The dreamer should look after himself in the near future.

Telephone If the dreamer is speaking on the telephone, he can expect success in the area under discussion. A ringing telephone in a dream means that a friend needs help. A silent telephone is symbolic of the fact that the dreamer feels discriminated against.

Telescope This indicates possible changes in the dreamer's career or professional life.

Temptation If the dreamer is being enticed by another person to perform a criminal act, the dream is a test and warning: Do not be tempted to walk forbidden paths in real life!

Tennis This is a sign that the dreamer feels the need to be popular and socially successful.

Tent This symbolizes protection and security. In the future, the dreamer will not face worry or disappointment.

Theater This shows that the dreamer has a strong desire to break his routine and bring his talents and creativity to the fore.

Thigh A thigh signifies recovery from a disease or the end of health problems.

Thimble This is a symbol of unrealistic, unrealizable ambitions.

Thorn This signifies that someone in the dreamer's

Dream Interpretation

environment is plotting against him and seeking to harm him.

Thread A torn thread indicates disappointment or loss brought about by the compassionate character of the dreamer.

Ticket Buying, receiving or handing someone a ticket indicates that a problem that has been bothering the dreamer lately will soon be solved.

Tin This is a warning that deceitful people surround the dreamer.

Toad The toad is a symbol of corruption. The dream warns against being tempted to engage in impure acts.

Toast This is a sign of a successful and enjoyable family life.

Tobacco Tobacco in any form, whether the dreamer or another person in the dream is smoking, indicates that the dreamer's problems will soon be solved, and that his character is conciliatory and moderate.

Tomato The dreamer has a need for social involvement.

Torture This expresses a vague fear or unbridled feelings of jealousy.

Tower If the dreamer sees himself standing at the top of a high building, it means that he will suffer financial difficulties, but will have a life full of happiness. Climbing a tower in a dream indicates problems in business. Climbing down a rope from a tower means economic success and prosperity.

Toys Clean, well-kept toys are a sign of happiness and joy for the dreamer. Broken toys signify difficult and sad times.

Trap If the dreamer falls into a trap, it indicates that he is a suspicious type, suspicious even of those who do not deserve it. If the dreamer himself laid the trap, it is a sign that he will soon lose a court case.

Trees Trees in bloom are a sign of a new love. Bare trees indicate marital problems.

Triangle This shows that there is a conflict in the dreamer's mind, usually connected with choosing a marriage partner.

Trumpet If a trumpet is heard in a dream, it signifies a change for the better. If the dreamer himself is playing the trumpet, it means he will succeed in overcoming difficulties that face him.

Tunnel Driving through a tunnel signifies a lack of confidence. If the dreamer sees himself trapped in a tunnel, it means that he is trying to shirk responsibility.

Turtle This predicts disappointment in one's love life.

Twins This means that the dreamer will make a decision that will not bring about the anticipated results.

𝒰

Ugliness This signifies only good things for the dreamer.

Ulcer (stomach) An ulcer is an indication of dissatisfaction as well as embarrassment which manifests itself in day-to-day life.

Umbrella An open umbrella symbolizes happiness, success and love of life.

Unicorn This mythical animal is connected to virginity and sexuality in the dreamer's life.

Uniform (clothing) If a uniform appears in a dream (on condition that it is not the dreamer who is wearing it), it signifies that the dreamer has been blessed with peace, tranquillity and true love by the people around him.

University This is a dream that bodes well: It indicates ambition and the desire for achievements, as well as a high level of success in all areas of life.

Vacation This indicates that the dreamer's life is about to change for the better, becoming calmer and more peaceful.

Vagina Dreaming about a vagina has a sexual interpretation which depends on the character of the dreamer.

Valley This is a sign that there will be a change in place of residence.

Vampire This signifies the dreamer's lack of self-confidence.

Vase This indicates that the dreamer is egocentric and only cares about his own good, and that the dreamer must demonstrate a higher degree of empathy and sensitivity toward others.

Vegetables Eating vegetables in a dream reflects the dreamer's careful nature: He does not like to take unnecessary risks.

Vegetation Dreaming about green vegetation is a good sign: The dreamer can expect exciting surprises or good news.

Velvet This signifies problems, arguments and domestic quarrels.

Victory This is a warning against taking sides in an argument in which the dreamer has very little knowledge of the subject at hand.

Village If the dreamer sees himself in an unknown village, there will be changes in his life in the near future.

Vine A vine with grapes indicates hard work that will result in prosperity and great success.

Vinegar This symbolizes jealousy, or that one of the dreamer's principal traits is jealousy which may make him suffer throughout his life.

Vineyard This signifies success in the economic field and particularly in the field of romance.

Violence This is an indication of pressure, anxiety or fear of the person or factor that the dreamer encounters in his dream.

Violets These indicate a love of the good life, hedonism and the pursuit of pleasure.

Violin If one hears a violin in a dream, it means the dreamer is becoming increasingly popular in social circles. If a violin string snaps, it signifies that the dreamer is a peace-maker. Tuning a violin indicates an imminent love affair.

Voices Hearing voices in a dream (without seeing their source) means that the dreamer will soon experience feelings of distress, sadness or depression.

Volcano The dreamer harbors an urgent need to control his emotions.

Vomiting This reflects an uneasy conscience. The dreamer is tormented because his actions were not pure.

Vote If the dreamer's vote is the deciding vote, it signifies a lack of confidence, a low self-image, and an impractical nature.

Voting Voting with a ballot attests to the dreamer's need for social involvement and the desire to be influential.

Vow This is a sign of an improvement in business and in one's financial situation.

Vulture Dreaming about a vulture (or any bird of prey) is a sign that a cold and ruthless enemy threatens the dreamer.

Wages Receiving wages in a dream indicates that without the dreamer's knowledge, someone is causing him harm and undermining him.

Waiter/Waitress This shows that the dreamer has an ambitious personality, and is striving to improve his financial situation.

Waking If the dreamer dreams that he is being awakened from sleep, a close and beloved person is about to appear and bring him much joy.

Walking Walking along a long, unbroken path indicates that the dreamer must cope with problems in his life. A brisk, steady walk means that he will overcome all the obstacles along his way.

Wall If the wall is solid and erect, the dream represents a warning against danger. If the wall is crumbling and falling, it actually symbolizes protection, and the dreamer will not be harmed.

Wallet If the dreamer finds a wallet, it indicates prosperity and financial success. The loss of a wallet predicts disappointment and frustration.

Walnut This is a sign of marriage to a rich partner. Eating walnuts in a dream indicates that the dreamer is wasteful and extravagant.

War If the dreamer declares war, it signifies success in the areas of business and economics. If he is a witness to war, it means that he must avoid actions that might endanger him, and only act following careful consideration.

Wasp If the dreamer sees a wasp, it means that bad news is on the way.

Water Drinking clear water is a sign of success, happiness and abundance. Drinking impure water warns against health problems. Dreaming about playing in water signifies that the dreamer is given a lot of love by those around him. Stormy waters indicate problems on the path to economic independence.

Waterfall This means that the great efforts the dreamer has made will not bear fruit. If the dreamer sees another individual swimming under the waterfall, it means that the person is in danger.

Dream Interpretation

Watermelon This symbolizes superstition, and reflects hidden fears and concealed anxiety.

Wax This warns against wastefulness and extravagance.

Wedding Dreaming about a wedding usually expresses the dreamer's wish. When a bachelor dreams about his own wedding, it means that unpleasant news is on its way. If a bachelor dreams of another person's wedding, it means that a period of happiness awaits him. If a married person dreams about a stranger's wedding, it means that he is jealous of his spouse.

Whale This is a sign that the dreamer is deprived of maternal love.

Wheat This symbolizes abundance, success and material wealth.

Whistle This means that ill-intentioned people are spreading malicious gossip about him.

Widowed If a dreamer dreams about being widowed from his spouse, this ensures a long life for his partner. An unmarried person who dreams about being widowed may expect marriage in the future.

Wig This is a sign of a lack of confidence in one's love life, and a struggle in making choices in romance.

Wildness/Raging If the dreamer participates in a wild, unruly event causing him to panic, it predicts financial difficulties in the near future.

Will Writing a will in a dream is actually a sign of a long and happy life.

Willow Dreaming of a willow has a painful significance: Mistakes made in the family context cannot be rectified.

Wind A strong wind, one that causes the dreamer anxiety, is a sign that he will find it difficult to cope with everyday life. If the strong wind does not frighten him, it shows that he will be able to cope with problems easily and successfully.

Window If the dreamer is gazing out of a window, this means that he will be reconciled with someone with whom he has quarreled. If another person is looking at the dreamer through a window, it warns of malicious gossip.

Wine The interpretation of wine in a dream depends on the particular culture: Some interpret wine as a sign of abundance, while others see it as a symbol of drunkenness and failure. Usually it means that the dreamer can expect family celebrations.

Winter Wintry weather indicates success in the near future. A dream about winter is sometimes interpreted as a sign of family problems, particularly parent-child relationships.

Witch Bad news can be expected soon.

Wolf The appearance of a wolf in any form in a dream signifies bad news. The news will be even more awful if the dream is about a pack of wolves.

Workshop This indicates that the dreamer will be able to achieve all to which he aspires. Any task that he undertakes will be a success.

Worm This means the same as a dream about a snake, but to a lesser degree. (See Snake.)

Writing If the dreamer is writing a letter, it means that a letter will arrive. If others are writing a letter, the dreamer will quarrel with someone who is close to him.

X-ray This signifies fear of poor health or serious financial problems.

Yeast This indicates a good life, abundance and a satisfying economic situation.

Zebra

This signifies that the dreamer will suffer from a severe illness or fatal accident in the future.

Zodiac This is a symbol of prosperity and economic and social success, following a great deal of effort and hard work.

Zoo Visiting a zoo is a sign of a good and successful future.